SAINTS
FOR BOYS

Written by Solveig Muu
Illustrations by Mi

TABLE OF CONTENTS

Library of Congress Control Number: 2011919882
ISBN 1-936020-57-7

SAINT JOSEPH

Feast Day: March 19

Patron of a Happy Home and the Universal Church

Joseph was a young carpenter from the town of Nazareth. He was engaged to Mary. Before they lived together, the Angel Gabriel appeared to Mary, telling her that God had chosen her to be the mother of His son. Mary accepted, and at that moment became the Mother of God.

In a dream, an angel told Joseph, "Joseph, son of David, do not be afraid to take Mary into your home. It is through the Holy Spirit that this child has been conceived in her. She will bear a son and you are to name him Jesus, because he will save his people from their sins." When Joseph awoke, he did all the angel had said, and took Mary into his home.

They journeyed to Bethlehem, where Jesus was born. King Herod wanted to kill him, because he was afraid Jesus would take away his kingdom. An angel spoke to Joseph in a dream, "Get up, take the child and his mother, and flee to Egypt! Stay there until I tell you." Joseph arose quickly and took Jesus and Mary and left that night for Egypt. After Herod died, they returned to Nazareth, where Joseph and Mary raised Jesus. Joseph taught Jesus to be strong and good, and he died before Jesus left Nazareth to begin his ministry.

SAINT JOHN THE BAPTIST

Feast Day: June 24

Patron of Baptism

Zechariah was the husband of Elizabeth, who was the Virgin Mary's cousin. Elizabeth and Zechariah were very old, and had never been able to have any children.

One day the angel Gabriel appeared to Zechariah and said, "Do not be afraid! Your wife Elizabeth will bear a son, and you shall call his name John. Many will rejoice at his birth. He will be filled with the Holy Spirit, and he will turn the hearts of many of the people of Israel to the Lord their God. He will prepare the way for the Lord."

John grew and became strong in spirit, and he lived in the desert until God called him to begin his ministry. John preached the coming of the Savior and baptized many repentant converts in the waters of the Jordan River. The people thought that John might be the coming Messiah, but he told everyone that he was sent to prepare the way for one who "is mightier than I."

Finally, John baptized Jesus. He said, "Behold the Lamb of God, who takes away the sin of the world." After that, King Herod arrested John and then had him beheaded. Saint John the Baptist gave his life for Jesus, his Lord.

SAINT PETER THE APOSTLE

Feast Day: June 29

Patron of Fishermen

Saint Peter, who was born with the name of Simon, was from a town called Bethsaida near the Sea of Galilee. He and his brother Andrew were fishermen by trade when they met Jesus. One day, Jesus told them, "Follow Me, and I will make you fishers of men." The two brothers left their boat and their father and followed Jesus.

Jesus later changed Simon's name when He said, "You are Peter, and on this rock I will build My Church." He then gave Peter the keys to the kingdom of heaven. Peter was our first Pope, Christ's representative on earth, and the shepherd of the Catholic Church. After Jesus ascended into heaven and the Holy Spirit came down upon Mary and the apostles at Pentecost, Peter guided the Church as Jesus had commanded him.

Peter journeyed to Rome to work along with Saint Paul to bring the Gospel to the whole world and to build up the Church, the Body of Christ. He wrote two Letters, known as Epistles, to all Christians. Saint Peter did not think he was worthy to die in the same way as Jesus, so he was crucified upside down by the Emperor Nero and buried on Vatican Hill.

SAINT JUDE THADDEUS

Feast Day: October 28

Patron of Desperate Cases

Saint Jude, known as Thaddeus, was the nephew of Mary and Joseph, and a cousin of our Lord. He was the brother of the apostle James the Less. As a young man, Saint Jude knew Jesus well, and left everything to follow Him.

At Pentecost, Saint Jude, along with Mother Mary and the other disciples of Jesus, was filled with the Holy Spirit. Tongues like fire rested on their heads, as the Holy Spirit gave the disciples the grace and the fervent desire to reach out to the lost of the world with the message of God's love. That is why Saint Jude is often pictured with a tongue of fire on his head.

Saint Jude is pictured wearing an image of Jesus because through the power of Jesus' name he healed a king suffering from leprosy. Saint Jude also wrote a Letter, or Epistle, that we find in the New Testament. He encourages us to keep strong in our faith even when it is not easy.

The two apostles, Saints Simon and Jude, labored as missionaries in the country of Armenia, where they suffered martyrdom. Saint Jude's relics today are honored in Saint Peter's basilica in Rome.

SAINT PAUL

Feast Day: June 29
Patron of Writers

Saint Paul was born Saul of Tarsus to Jewish parents. He spent much time studying the laws of God and the books of men. Saul did not believe in Jesus and thought that Christians should be persecuted and put to death. He even held the robes of those who stoned Saint Stephen, the first martyr to die for Jesus in the early days of the Church.

One day, as Saul was traveling on the road to Damascus to find and arrest Christians, a brilliant light flashed around him. Saul fell to the ground and he heard a voice saying, "Saul, Saul, why are you persecuting Me?" The light blinded Saul for several days, but he always remembered the vision of Jesus that he saw in that bright light. Saul repented of his sins, was baptized, and changed his name to Paul.

Saint Paul started many churches and preached the Gospel everywhere he went. He endured many sufferings for the sake of Christ, and wrote many Letters, or Epistles, which are in the New Testament. Saint Paul was put into prison in Rome, where he was beheaded as a martyr. Saint Paul is known today as the "Apostle to the Gentiles."

SAINT CHRISTOPHER

Feast Day: July 25

Patron of Travelers

Saint Christopher was a very strong man who lived long ago. He was so strong that he carried travelers on his back across a nearby river. Christopher wanted to serve the greatest king of all. He served his own king until he heard about Jesus, the King of Kings. He searched all over the world, but couldn't find Him.

One cold stormy night, a little Child knocked on the door of Christopher's cottage and asked him for a ride across the river. As they crossed the raging torrent, the Child grew heavier and heavier until Christopher thought they would both be swept away by the rushing waters. "Who are you?" Christopher asked.

The Child answered, "I am Jesus, and I bear on my shoulders the weight of the world." Christopher knelt in adoration, and received his name which means Christ-Bearer. After that night, Christopher preached about Christ to all who came his way, and he died as a martyr for the Child he had carried with so much love.

Saint Christopher has come to be known through the ages as the patron of all who journey, so that, wherever people may travel, Saint Christopher should go with them.

SAINT AUGUSTINE OF HIPPO

Feast Day: August 28

Patron of Theologians

Augustine was born in Africa in the year 354. His mother Monica was a Christian whose love and goodness influenced Augustine's father to become a Christian shortly before his death. Saint Monica raised Augustine in the Christian faith, but Augustine turned from this faith to the pleasures of the world. His mother prayed every day that God would help her son.

God heard Saint Monica's prayer and gave Augustine the grace to accept Jesus as his Savior. When he was 33 years old, Augustine was baptized by Saint Ambrose. Augustine turned to Jesus with all his heart. He used his money and talents to help other people come to know Jesus and His Gospel. "Our hearts are made for Thee, O Lord," he wrote, "and restless shall they be, until they rest in Thee."

Augustine became the bishop of Hippo, in Africa, and lived there for many years, fighting the good fight of the Gospel and writing much. He became one of the greatest saints and teachers of the Church, and finally, he went home to be in heaven with his beloved mother and father and his dear Lord Jesus, when he died in the year 430.

SAINT PATRICK

Feast Day: March 17
Patron of Ireland

Patrick was born around 389. Irish raiders captured him and took him to Ireland when he was a teenager. Although he was treated harshly, Patrick stayed close to Jesus and the Catholic Faith. Six years later he escaped, and after many trials made his way home. Patrick dreamed of all the children of Ireland stretching out their hands and crying to him for relief. God showed Patrick that he was to return to bring the Gospel of Jesus and His wonderful love to Ireland.

Patrick was made Bishop of Ireland, and he brought the Faith everywhere despite the hostility of the Druid priests.

Saint Patrick established many monasteries for men and women. He restored sight to the blind, health to the sick, and raised the dead to life. He died on March 17th.

Saint Patrick's Breastplate

Christ be with me, Christ within me,
Christ behind me, Christ before me,
Christ beside me, Christ to win me,
Christ to comfort and restore me.
Christ beneath me, Christ above me,
Christ in the hearts of all who love me,
Christ in the mouth of friend and stranger. Amen.

SAINT BENEDICT

Feast Day: July 11

Patron of Europe

Saint Benedict was born in Italy in 480 A.D. Educated at Rome, Benedict became so upset by the wickedness of the Romans that he fled to a cave, where he lived as a hermit for three years. Disciples gathered around Benedict, attracted by his holiness and miraculous gifts. Benedict and his brother monks moved to the top of a mountain in a place called Monte Cassino. He destroyed a pagan temple, brought the people back to Christianity, and founded the monastery that drew many men who wanted to follow Jesus and serve others.

Benedict organized the monks and wrote his famous Rule to help keep the monks together and to help them grow as a family of God. His Rule helped many monks in Europe for centuries to come, as they kept alive the light of faith and learning through the Middle Ages. Their motto was: Pray and Work.

Saint Benedict's holiness and gifts remind us that God loves each of us so much that He continues to send holy ones to help us follow Him. When he died, Benedict was buried with his beloved twin sister, Saint Scholastica.

SAINT FRANCIS OF ASSISI

Feast Day: October 4

Patron of Animals

Saint Francis, perhaps the best-loved of all the saints, was born in Assisi, Italy in 1181. Thanks to his wealthy father, young Francis enjoyed a life of luxury and fine clothes.

One day, Jesus spoke to Francis from the crucifix in the little church of San Damiano: "Go, rebuild My house." Francis gave his clothes back to his father, put on an old robe, and went about as a barefoot beggar, caring for the sick and preaching peace and God's love for all creation. He thought of the animals as his brothers and sisters.

One day, by God's grace, Francis hugged a sick leper, and felt a great love for him in his soul. Others joined Francis in his care for the sick and lepers and thus the Franciscan order was born. Clare of Assisi, a dear friend, also joined Francis and his brothers, and in 1212 she founded the Order of the Poor Clares. Francis prepared the first outdoor Christmas Nativity in a town called Greccio. He also became friends with a wolf and had him stop stealing food from people in the town of Gubbio.

God blessed Francis with the wounds of Jesus in his hands and feet, and Saint Francis died two years later, with the words, "Welcome, Sister Death!"

SAINT ANTHONY OF PADUA

Feast Day: June 13

Patron of the Poor

Saint Anthony was born on August 15, 1195, to a wealthy family in Portugal. He became a Franciscan at the age of 26, when he beheld the bodies of the first five Franciscan martyrs returned from North Africa for burial.

Saint Anthony loved to teach others about Jesus and the Catholic faith. He especially loved to preach to those who did not believe. His secret was simply to repeat to himself the name of our Blessed Mother Mary as he preached. He attracted huge crowds, and was so successful that he is called the "Hammer of Heretics."

One day, when people would not listen to him, Saint Anthony went to preach to the fish, which gathered at the banks of the lake and listened attentively to the Word of God. Another time, after he prayed, a brother who had run away returned with a book he had stolen, and so we pray to Saint Anthony to help us find lost articles.

One day a friend saw Anthony holding the infant Jesus in his arms. Perhaps it was Jesus' way of thanking Saint Anthony for his love and goodness to all, especially the poor. Saint Anthony died in 1231, at the age of 36.

SAINT THOMAS AQUINAS

Feast Day: January 28

Patron of Students

Thomas Aquinas was born into a noble Italian family in 1226. When he was 17, he joined the Dominican Order, against his family's wishes. His brothers kidnapped him and held him prisoner for two years in their castle. However, Thomas escaped and went to Germany to study under Saint Albert the Great. He became a priest and was sent to Paris, where he taught philosophy and theology for many years.

Saint Thomas deeply loved Our Lord in the Blessed Sacrament. He wrote special prayers and hymns for the feast of Corpus Christi—the Body of Christ. His greatest work is a summary of the theology of the Church, called the Summa Theologica.

One day God gave Saint Thomas a special experience of His presence. After this, Saint Thomas stopped writing, saying his writing was like "so much straw" when compared to God's glory. Saint Thomas Aquinas died in 1274. He was named the Angelic Doctor, or Teacher, because the Church considered his teachings to be as wise and as holy as those of the angels in heaven.

SAINT IGNATIUS LOYOLA

Feast Day: July 31

Patron of Educators and Retreatants

Saint Ignatius was born at Loyola, Spain, in the year 1491. After being wounded in battle, he laid down his weapons and became a soldier in the army of the Lord.

Ignatius went to study at the University of Paris, where several young men joined him to serve Christ. They called themselves the "Companions of Jesus," but people began to call them Jesuits—the Society of Jesus. The little group of men committed their service to the Pope. "The Companions," said Ignatius, "are ready to do any work or go anywhere in the world for God's greater glory." The Jesuits became famous teachers, and even though their popularity grew, they remained active among the poor, living and teaching as soldiers of Christ.

Saint Ignatius suffered many trials, but he trusted in God, and composed his famous "Spiritual Exercises," to help all people discover God's Will for them. The Jesuits served at the Council of Trent, helping Catholics grow in their true faith. Saint Ignatius died on July 31st, 1556.

SAINT FRANCIS XAVIER

Feast Day: December 3
Patron of Missionaries

Francis Xavier was born to noble parents in the Basque region of Spain in 1506. As a young man, he did very well in studies and sports, winning many prizes for his accomplishments. Xavier moved on to the University of Paris, where he met Saint Ignatius of Loyola, who won him over to Christ. He and five other companions helped Saint Ignatius found the Society of Jesus—the Jesuits—and he was ordained a priest in 1537.

Saint Ignatius sent Father Xavier to the India, where he preached the Gospel and baptized tens of thousands of people from there to Japan. Many people tried to discourage him, but Saint Francis knew that the light of the Gospel is stronger than the darkness of evil. He set out for China, willing to risk his life if it should come to that, but he died within sight of that great country in 1552.

Saint Francis Xavier is considered the greatest missionary since Saint Paul. He was canonized with Saint Ignatius Loyola in 1622, and in 1904, Pope Saint Pius X proclaimed Saint Francis Xavier, along with Saint Therese of Lisieux, as co-patron of all foreign missions.

SAINT MARTIN DE PORRES

Feast Day: November 3

Patron of Barbers and Interracial Justice

Saint Martin de Porres was born at Lima, Peru, in 1579. His father was a Spanish gentleman, and his mother was a black woman freed from slave-owners in Panama. When he was 15, Martin entered the Dominican Friary at Lima and served as a farm laborer and barber.

After Martin studied medicine, he worked with the poor, caring for the sick and dying. They greeted him with open arms. Others, however, including some of his fellow monks, insulted him because he was black.

Saint Martin's exceptional kindness and purity eventually won over the monks and they joined him in his work. When they were worried or sick, Martin prayed by their side and asked God to heal them. God endowed Saint Martin with many graces, including humility, gentleness, wisdom, and healing. He opened many orphanages and raised money for children by begging on the streets.

Saint Martin de Porres loved all of God's creation, caring for dogs, cats, and other animals. He was a close friend of Saint Rose of Lima, and he died on November 3, 1639.

THANK YOU, DEAR GOD!

Dear God, thank You for giving me the gift of life. I like being alive! Thank You for the gift of my Baptism, for giving me new life in Jesus as Your child. Thank You, dear Heavenly Father, for inviting me to know You, to love You, and to serve You.

Thank You for my family, friends, and teachers who help me grow to be a kind and good person. Thank You for Your Saints, my heavenly family, who show me by their lives how to live a life pleasing to You. They received Your love and grace, and loved and served others in return.

May I come to know the Saints and to be filled with their joy. Fill me with Your Holy Spirit, that I may also become holy by loving You, myself, and others. In Jesus' name I pray. Amen.

Dear Mother Mary, Queen of all Saints, pray for us!